Toddler's Toy Townhouse Play Set
Full-size
WOOD TOY PATTERNS

Patterns include the toy townhouse, little people, pup, sports cars, trees, shrubs and a houseful of furniture. Even a gas station!

1/24 SCALE

14-3/8" HIGH
29-1/4" WIDE
29-1/4" DEEP

John W. Lewman
Cynthia A. Lewman

TODDLER'S TOY TOWNHOUSE PLAY SET
FULL-SIZE
WOOD TOY PATTERNS

Toymaker Press is dedicated to providing you with the patterns and plans you need to develop your skills as a toymaker. We welcome your comments and any suggestions about this collection or any other subject.
Email: johnlewman@toymakerpress.com

©2010
Toymaker Press, Inc.
All rights reserved
First edition

Printed in China

Due to different conditions, tools, and individual skills, Toymaker Press assumes no responsibility for any damages, injuries suffered, or losses incurred as a result of following the information published in this book. Before beginning any project review instructions carefully. If any doubts or questions remain consult local experts or authorities.

Toymaker Press, Inc.
Shawnee, KS 66216
www.toymakerpress.com
phone: 913-962-4714

ISBN 978-1-61658-813-7

9 781616 588137

© Toymaker Press, Inc. 2010

TODDLER'S TOY TOWNHOUSE
Full-size
1/24 SCALE

Wood Toy Patterns

TABLE OF CONTENTS

You can build as many Toddler's Townhouse Play Sets as you like. Toys built from these toy plans and patterns are royalty free. Each and every toy can be built in any quantity for your personal or commercial use.

Toymaker Press toy plans, patterns and plan sets are copyrighted and cannot be distributed or shared for free by any person or business for any commercial purpose without the approval and written consent of Toymaker Press.

Toddler's Toy Townhouse

FULL SIZE PATTERNS PAGES 12-17

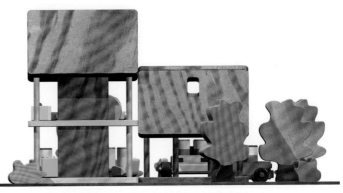

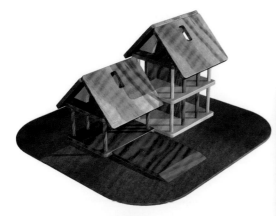

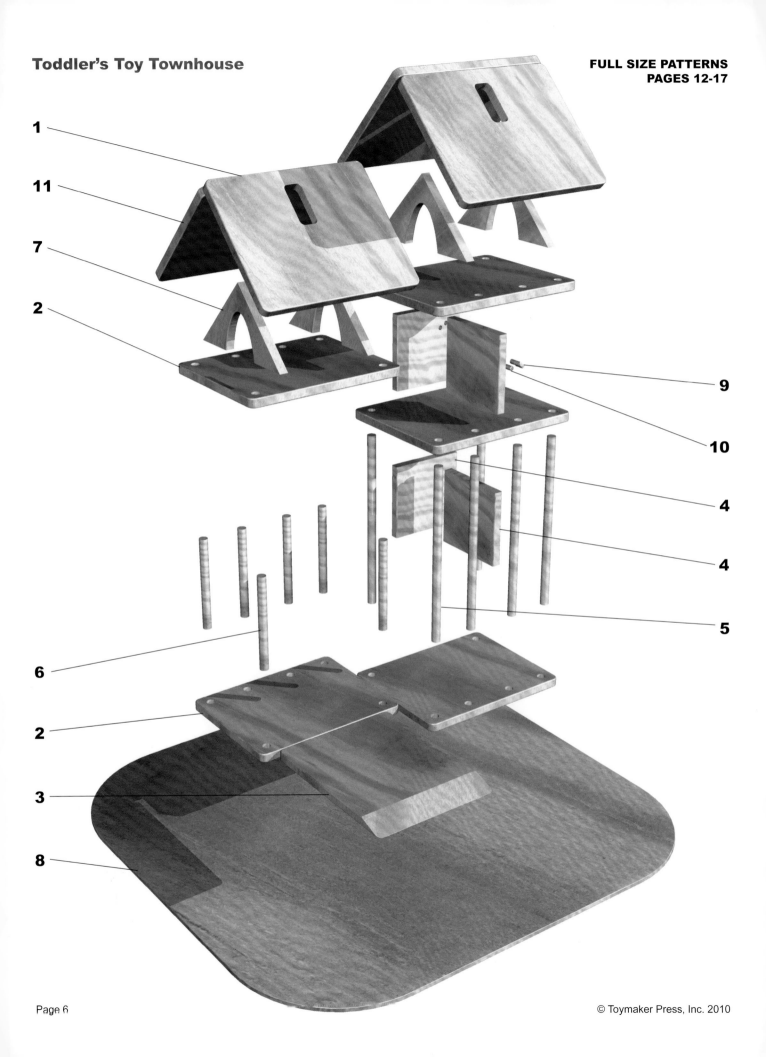

Toddler's Toy Townhouse

**FULL SIZE PATTERNS
PAGES, 12-17**

1

11

7

2

9

10

4

4

5

6

2

3

8

TODDLER'S TOY TOWNHOUSE PARTS LIST (list also shown on page 17)

NOTE: All house panels are sawn from 1/2" plywood. House and garage posts are sawn from 1/2" dowels.

1.	SKYLIGHT ROOF	MAKE 2	1/2" X 7-1/2" X 9-1/2"	PLYWOOD
2.	FLOOR	MAKE 5	1/2" X 7-1/2" X 9-1/2"	PLYWOOD
3.	DRIVEWAY	MAKE 1	1/2" X 7-1/2" X 9-1/2"	PLYWOOD
4.	WALL	MAKE 4	1/2" X 4-1/4" X 4-7/16"	PLYWOOD
5.	HOUSE POST	MAKE 6	10" X 1/2" diameter	DOWEL
6.	GARAGE POST	MAKE 6	5-1/4" X 1/2" diameter	DOWEL
7.	ROOF GABLE	MAKE 4	1/2" X 3-3/4" X 7-1/2"	PLYWOOD
8.	LANDSCAPE	MAKE 1	1/4" X 29-1/4" X 29-1/4"	PLYWOOD
9.	SHOWER NOZZLE	MAKE 1	1/2" X 1/4" diameter	DOWEL
10.	SHOWER HANDLE	MAKE 2	3/8" X 1/4" diameter	DOWEL
11.	SOLID ROOF	MAKE 2	1/2" X 7-1/2" X 9-1/2"	PLYWOOD

The Toddler's Townhouse and Garage are both built with the post and slide type of construction. The posts are first glued into the bottom floor then the second and third floors slide down the posts and are glued to the adjacent walls. Your Toddler's Townhouse can be built in a reasonable amount of time using this simple and unique assembly technique. Refer to patterns for hole placement.

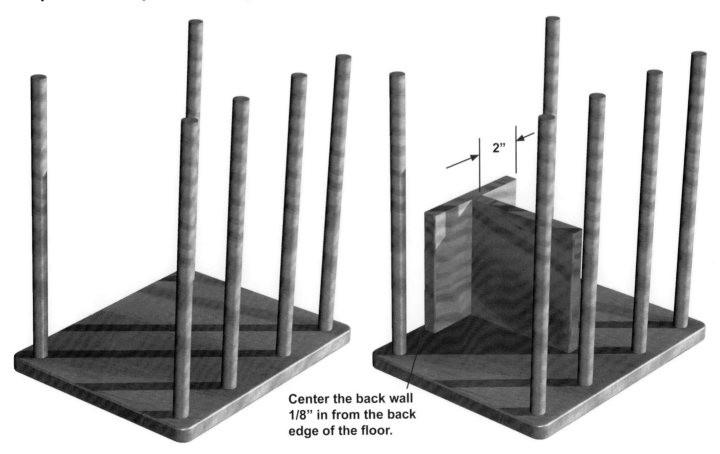

2"

Center the back wall
1/8" in from the back
edge of the floor.

1. Place the floor on a solid surface. Apply woodworker's glue to the end of each house post and insert the posts firmly into each of the holes in the floor. Let glue dry before proceeding.

2. First glue the 2 walls together as shown. The inner wall is on-center with the outside wall. Once dry, glue the 2 piece wall assembly to the floor. Let glue dry before proceeding.

3. Apply glue to top edges of first floor walls. Align second floor post holes with top of posts and slide floor down tightly against the first floor walls. No glue is required in post holes.

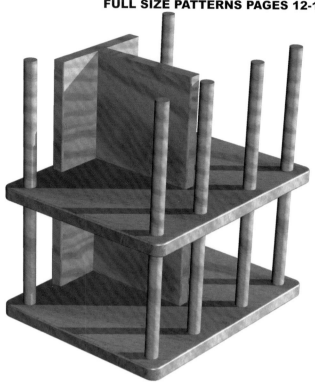

4. Glue the second floor walls together and let dry. Next glue the wall assembly to the second floor. Let dry. The back wall of the wall assembly is attached 1/8" from back edge of floor.

5. Apply glue to top edges of second floor walls. Align top floor post holes with top of posts and slide top floor down tightly against the second floor walls. No glue is required in post holes.

6. Next glue the roof gables into place at a position 1-3/4" in from each end of the top floor section. Let glued assembly dry completely before attaching the roof sections.

7. Glue the rear roof section to the roof gables. Let the roof section overhang the roof gables at the roof gable peak by 1/2" to allow for the front roof section to fit flush with the rear roof section.

8. Glue the front roof section to the roof gables and to the underside overlap of the rear roof section. The front roof section is designed to be flush with the front edge of the rear roof section.

9. Place garage floor section on a solid surface and glue the garage posts into the holes in the floor. The driveway is not glued into position until a later assembly step.

10. Glue the top floor of the garage assembly into place. The top floor assembly is flush with the top edge of the garage posts. The driveway is not glued into position until a later assembly step.

11. Glue the 2 garage roof gables into position at 1-3/4" in from the left and right edge of the garage second floor section. Let the glue on roof gables dry completely before proceeding.

12. Glue the rear roof section to the roof gables. Let the roof section overhang the roof gables at the roof gable peak by 1/2" to allow for the front roof section to fit flush with the rear roof section.

13. Glue the front roof section to the roof gables and to the underside overlap of the rear roof section. The front roof section is designed to be flush with the front edge of the rear roof section. Glue driveway into position on the landscape. See part 8 page 16.

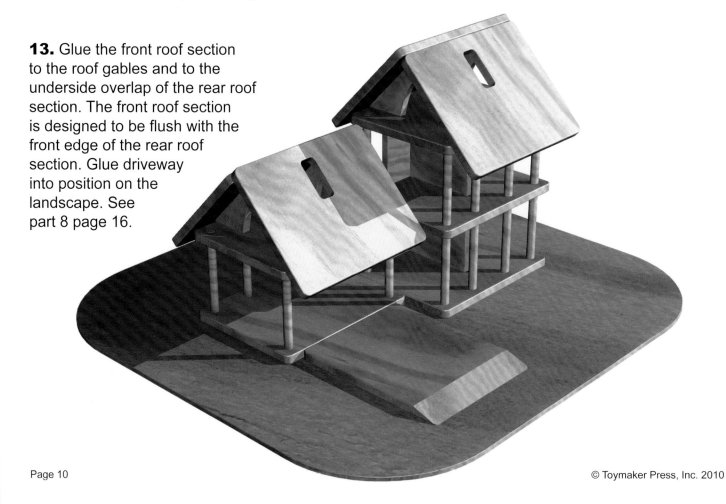

Toddler's Toy Townhouse

14. APPLYING FINISHING TOUCHES

The Toddler's Toy Townhouse is designed to be finished in natural wood or in bright toddler's colors.

For a natural wood look apply clear, non-toxic polyurethane. Sand the house with a fine grit sandpaper. Apply the first coat, let it dry thoroughly. Lightly sand first coat then apply 2 coats sanding between each. Following the final coat rub lightly with steel wool for a soft to the touch and feel to the surfaces.

Bright colors can be applied using non-toxic acrylic paints as solid colors or thinned to apply as a wash or stain prior to assembly. Do not apply paint to gluing surfaces. First sand all parts with a fine grit sandpaper. Apply first coat, let dry thoroughly. Sand first coat then apply 2 coats sanding between each coat. Following assembly rub the entire townhouse with steel wool for a soft to the touch feel on the surfaces.

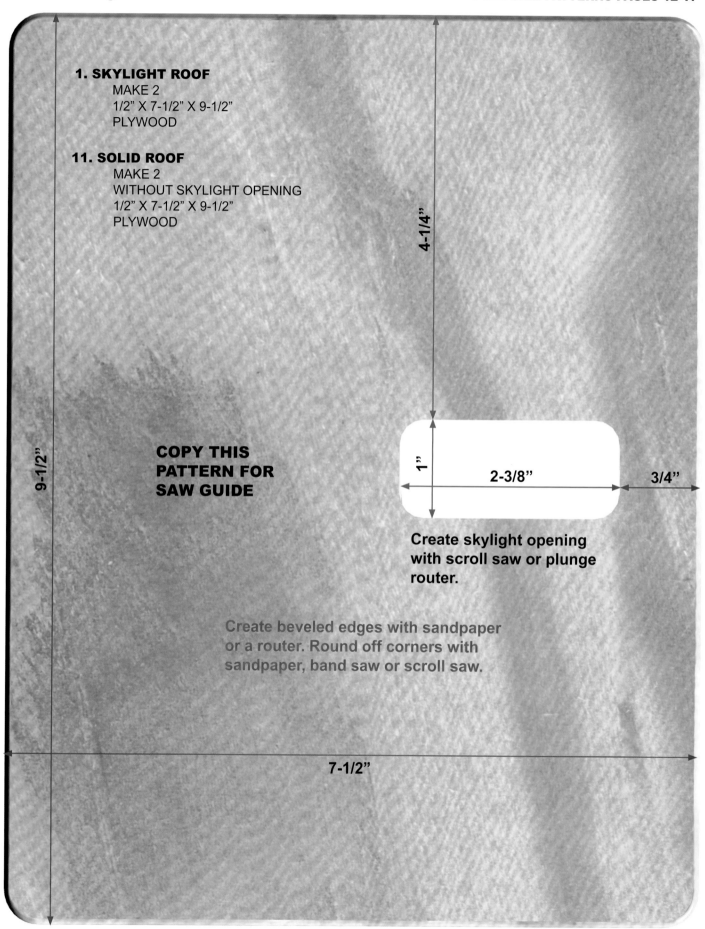

1. SKYLIGHT ROOF
MAKE 2
1/2" X 7-1/2" X 9-1/2"
PLYWOOD

11. SOLID ROOF
MAKE 2
WITHOUT SKYLIGHT OPENING
1/2" X 7-1/2" X 9-1/2"
PLYWOOD

COPY THIS PATTERN FOR SAW GUIDE

4-1/4"

9-1/2"

1"

2-3/8"

3/4"

Create skylight opening with scroll saw or plunge router.

Create beveled edges with sandpaper or a router. Round off corners with sandpaper, band saw or scroll saw.

7-1/2"

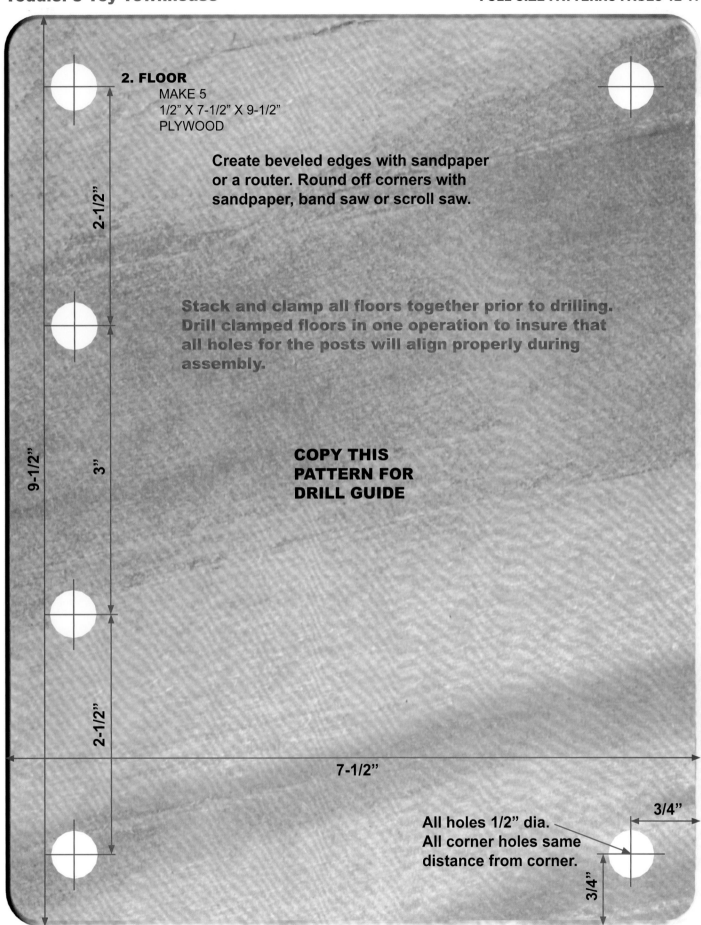

2. FLOOR
MAKE 5
1/2" X 7-1/2" X 9-1/2"
PLYWOOD

Create beveled edges with sandpaper
or a router. Round off corners with
sandpaper, band saw or scroll saw.

Stack and clamp all floors together prior to drilling.
Drill clamped floors in one operation to insure that
all holes for the posts will align properly during
assembly.

**COPY THIS
PATTERN FOR
DRILL GUIDE**

2-1/2"

3"

9-1/2"

2-1/2"

7-1/2"

3/4"

All holes 1/2" dia.
All corner holes same
distance from corner.

3/4"

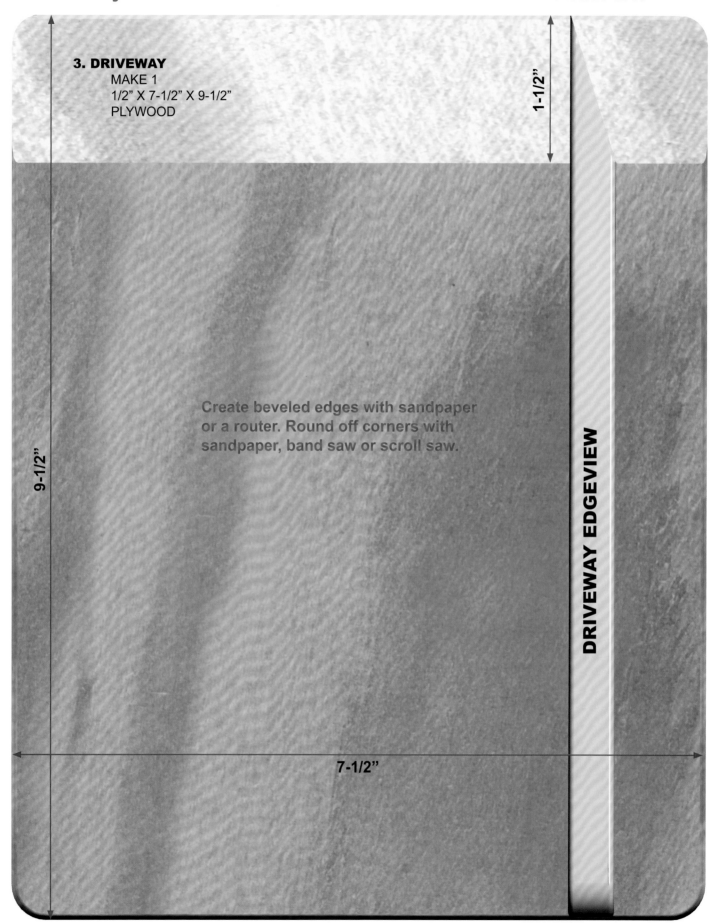

3. DRIVEWAY
MAKE 1
1/2" X 7-1/2" X 9-1/2"
PLYWOOD

1-1/2"

Create beveled edges with sandpaper
or a router. Round off corners with
sandpaper, band saw or scroll saw.

9-1/2"

DRIVEWAY EDGEVIEW

7-1/2"

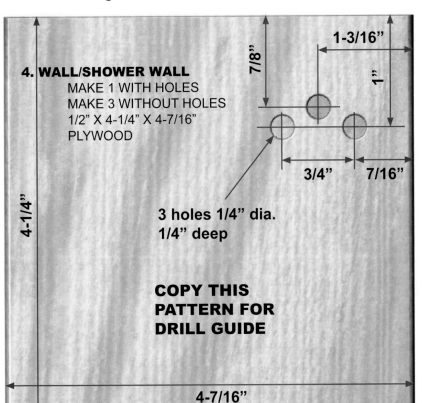

4. WALL/SHOWER WALL
MAKE 1 WITH HOLES
MAKE 3 WITHOUT HOLES
1/2" X 4-1/4" X 4-7/16"
PLYWOOD

7/8"

1-3/16"

1"

3/4"

7/16"

4-1/4"

3 holes 1/4" dia.
1/4" deep

**COPY THIS
PATTERN FOR
DRILL GUIDE**

4-7/16"

5. HOUSE POST
MAKE 6
10" X 1/2" diameter
DOWEL

6. GARAGE POST
MAKE 6
5-1/4" X 1/2" diameter
DOWEL

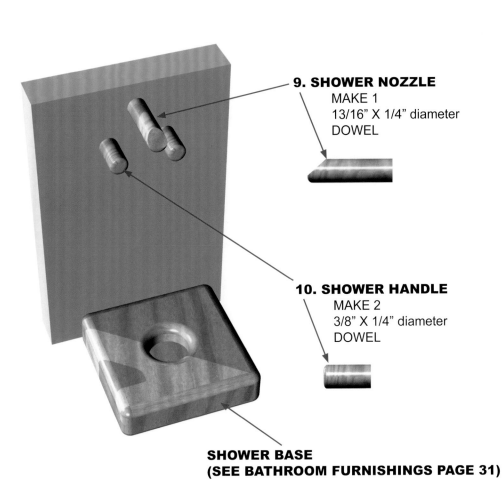

9. SHOWER NOZZLE
MAKE 1
13/16" X 1/4" diameter
DOWEL

10. SHOWER HANDLE
MAKE 2
3/8" X 1/4" diameter
DOWEL

**SHOWER BASE
(SEE BATHROOM FURNISHINGS PAGE 31)**

**FULL SIZE PATTERN FOR
LANDSCAPE CORNERS**

**COPY THIS PATTERN FOR
LANDSCAPE (4 CORNERS) SAW GUIDE**

6-3/4" RADIUS

Round off corners with band saw or
scroll saw and sandpaper.

8. LANDSCAPE
  MAKE 1
  1/4" X 29-1/4" X 29-1/4"
  PLYWOOD

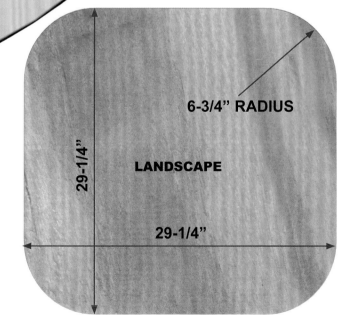

6-3/4" RADIUS

29-1/4"

LANDSCAPE

29-1/4"

Toddler's Toy Townhouse

7. ROOF GABLE
MAKE 4
1/2" X 3-3/4" X 7-1/2"
PLYWOOD

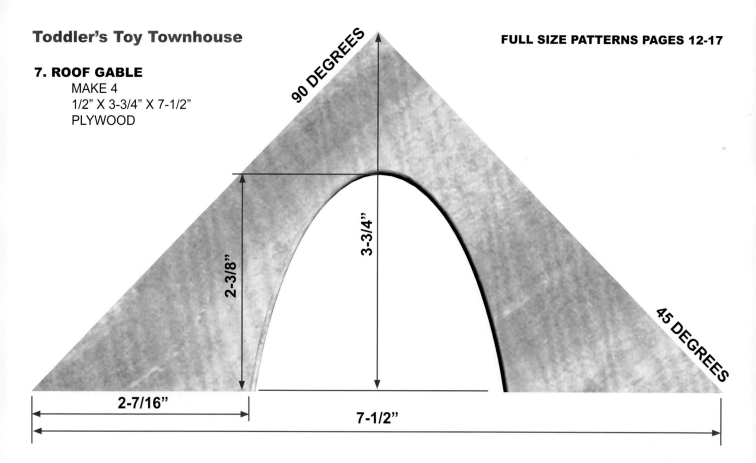

90 DEGREES

45 DEGREES

2-3/8"

3-3/4"

2-7/16"

7-1/2"

TODDLER'S TOY TOWNHOUSE PARTS LIST (copy of list on page 7)

NOTE: All house panels are sawn from 1/2" plywood. House and garage posts are sawn from 1/2" dowels.

#	Part	Make	Dimensions	Material
1.	SKYLIGHT ROOF	MAKE 2	1/2" X 7-1/2" X 9-1/2"	PLYWOOD
2.	FLOOR	MAKE 5	1/2" X 7-1/2" X 9-1/2"	PLYWOOD
3.	DRIVEWAY	MAKE 1	1/2" X 7-1/2" X 9-1/2"	PLYWOOD
4.	WALL	MAKE 4	1/2" X 4-1/4" X 4-7/16"	PLYWOOD
5.	HOUSE POST	MAKE 6	10" X 1/2" diameter	DOWEL
6.	GARAGE POST	MAKE 6	5-1/4" X 1/2" diameter	DOWEL
7.	ROOF GABLE	MAKE 4	1/2" X 3-3/4" X 7-1/2"	PLYWOOD
8.	LANDSCAPE	MAKE 1	1/4" X 29-1/4" X 29-1/4"	PLYWOOD
9.	SHOWER NOZZLE	MAKE 1	1/2" X 1/4" diameter	DOWEL
10.	SHOWER HANDLE	MAKE 2	3/8" X 1/4" diameter	DOWEL
11.	SOLID ROOF	MAKE 2	1/2" X 7-1/2" X 9-1/2"	PLYWOOD

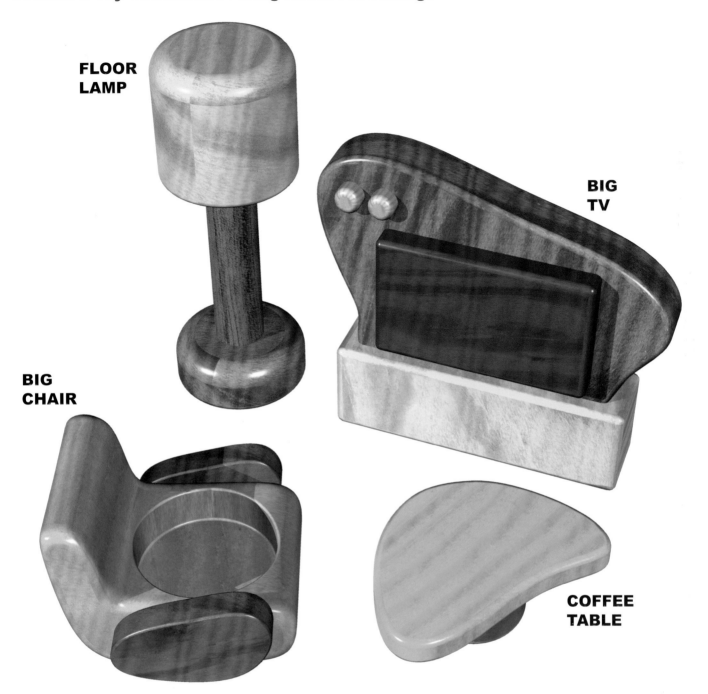

FLOOR LAMP

BIG TV

BIG CHAIR

COFFEE TABLE

APPLYING FINISHES TO FURNITURE

The Toddler's Toy Townhouse Living Room Furniture is designed to be finished in natural wood or in bright toddler's colors. **For a natural wood look** apply clear, non-toxic polyurethane. Sand furniture with a fine grit sandpaper. Apply first coat, let it dry thoroughly. Lightly sand first coat then apply 2 coats sanding between each. Following the final coat rub lightly with steel wool for a soft to the touch feel to the surfaces.

Bright colors can be applied using non-toxic acrylic paints as solid colors or thinned to apply as a wash or stain prior assembly. Do not apply paint to gluing surfaces. First sand all parts with a fine grit sandpaper.

Apply first coat, let it dry thoroughly. Sand first coat then apply 2 coats sanding between each coat. Following assembly rub each furniture piece with steel wool for a soft to the touch feel to the surfaces.

BIG TV

COPY THIS
PATTERN FOR
SAW AND DRILL
GUIDE

1. BACK PANEL
(1) 1/2" X 2-1/16" X 3-7/16"
PINE

2. TV KNOBS
(2) 1/4" diameter X 1/2"
DOWEL

3. TV SCREEN
(1) 1/4" X 1-1/4" X 2-1/8"
PINE

4. TV BASE
(1) 3/4" X 7/8" X 2-7/8"
PINE

1. Glue the back panel into position at 1/8" in from the front and back edge of the TV base. Let the glue dry completely before proceeding.

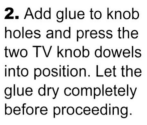

2. Add glue to knob holes and press the two TV knob dowels into position. Let the glue dry completely before proceeding.

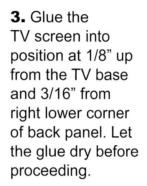

3. Glue the TV screen into position at 1/8" up from the TV base and 3/16" from right lower corner of back panel. Let the glue dry before proceeding.

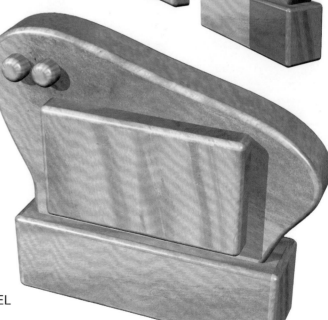

BIG TV PARTS LIST

1. BACK PANEL	(1)	1/2" X 2-1/16" X 3-7/16"	PINE
2. TV KNOBS	(2)	1/4" diameter X 1/2"	DOWEL
3. TV SCREEN	(1)	1/4" X 1-1/4" X 2-1/8"	PINE
4. TV BASE	(1)	3/4" X 7/8" X 2-7/8"	PINE

FLOOR LAMP

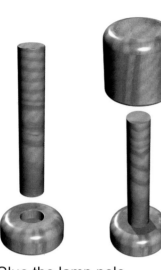

1. Glue the lamp pole into position in lamp base. Let the glue dry.

2. Add glue to lamp shade hole and press pole into position. Let the glue dry.

FLOOR LAMP PARTS LIST

1. LAMP SHADE	(1)	1-1/4" dia. X 1-3/16"	DOWEL
2. LAMP BASE	(1)	1-1/4" dia. X 7/16"	DOWEL
3. LAMP POLE	(1)	1/2" dia. X 3-1/16"	PINE

NOTE:
Shade hole 1/2" dia. X 1/2" DEEP

Base hole 1/2" dia. X 1/4" DEEP

1. LAMP SHADE
(1) 1-1/4" diameter X 1-3/16" DOWEL

2. LAMP BASE
(1) 1-1/4" diameter X 7/16" DOWEL

3. LAMP POLE (1) 1/2" dia. X 3-1/16" DOWEL

BIG CHAIR

1. Glue the right arm into position on chair base. Let the glue dry before next step.

2. Glue the left arm into position on chair base. Let the glue dry before next step.

3. Sand and finish the big chair with clear poly or bright colors and stains.

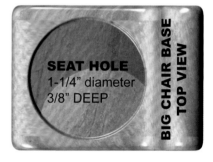

SEAT HOLE
1-1/4" diameter
3/8" DEEP

BIG CHAIR BASE TOP VIEW

COPY PATTERNS FOR SAW AND DRILL GUIDE

3. BIG CHAIR BASE
(1) 1-1/2" X 1-9/16" X 2-1/16"

BIG CHAIR PARTS LIST

1. LEFT ARM	(1)	1/4" X 13/16" X 1-3/8"	PINE
2. RIGHT ARM	(1)	1/4" X 13/16" X 1-3/8"	PINE
3. CHAIR BASE	(1)	1-1/2" X 1-9/16" X 2-1/16"	PINE

2. RIGHT ARM

1. LEFT ARM

COFFEE TABLE

**COPY THIS PATTERN FOR
SAW AND DRILL GUIDE**

1. Add glue to table base and press the base into position on bottom of table top. Let the glue dry before proceeding.

2. Sand edges to soften and finish with a polyurethane clearcoat or with non-toxic paints or stains.

1. TABLE TOP
(1) 1/4" X 1-1/2" X 2-1/4"   PINE

2. TABLE BASE
(1) 1/2" X 1" diameter DOWEL

COFFEE TABLE PARTS LIST

| 1. | TABLE TOP | (1) | 1/4" X 1-1/2" X 2-1/4" | PINE |
| 2. | TABLE BASE | (1) | 1/2" X 1" diameter | DOWEL |

**FULL SIZE PATTERNS
PAGES 23-25**

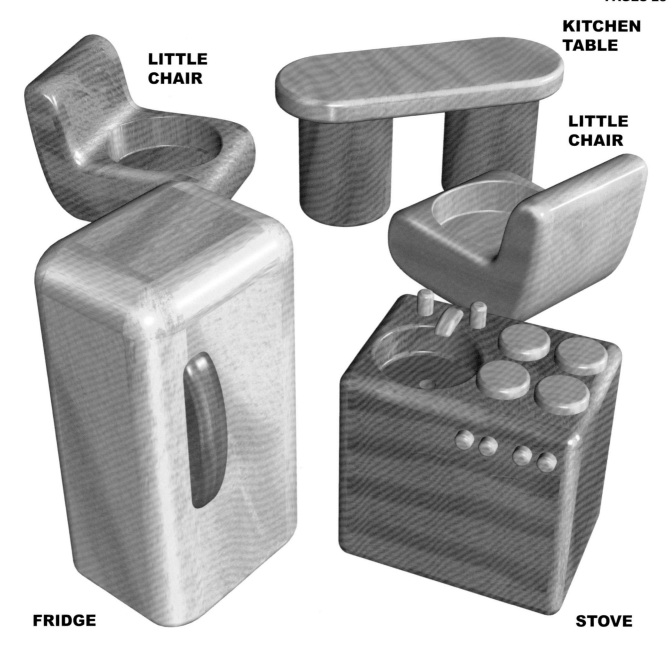

KITCHEN TABLE

LITTLE CHAIR

LITTLE CHAIR

FRIDGE

STOVE

APPLYING FINISHES TO THE KITCHEN APPLIANCES AND FURNISHINGS.

The Toddler's Toy Townhouse kitchen appliances and furnishings are designed to be finished in natural wood or in bright toddler's colors.

For a natural wood look apply clear, non-toxic polyurethane. Sand parts with a fine grit sandpaper. Lightly sand first coat then apply 2 coats sanding between each. Following the final coat rub lightly steel wool for a soft feel.

Bright colors can be applied using non-toxic acrylic paints as solid colors or thinned to apply as a wash or stain prior assembly.

Do not apply paint to gluing surfaces.

First sand all parts with a fine grit sandpaper. Apply first coat, let it dry thoroughly. Sand first coat then apply 2 coats sanding between each. Following assembly rub the each furnishing and appliance with steel wool for a soft to the touch feel to the surfaces.

LITTLE CHAIR

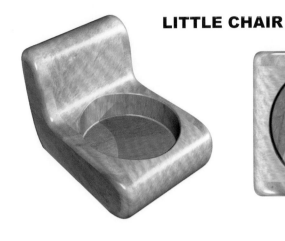

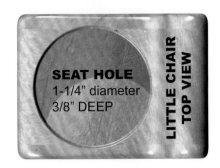

SEAT HOLE
1-1/4" diameter
3/8" DEEP

LITTLE CHAIR
TOP VIEW

**COPY
PATTERNS
FOR SAW
AND DRILL
GUIDE**

1. LITTLE CHAIR
(1) 1-1/2" x 1-9/16" x
2-1/16" PINE

FRIDGE

**Kids have lots of fun decorating the townhouse
furnishings with non-toxic paints, stains and crayons.**

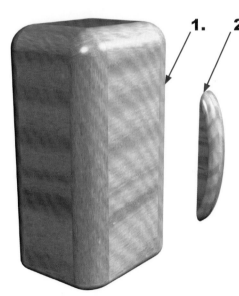

1.   2.

2. HANDLE
1-1/4" X 1/4" X 1/4"
PINE

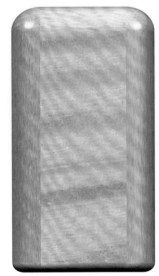

1. FRIDGE
1-1/4" X 1-1/2" X 2-3/4"
PINE

1. Add a small spot of glue to fridge handle and a spot of glue to the fridge where the handle is to be positioned.

2. Press handle into place on the fridge using the above drawing as a guide. Let dry before handling the toy.

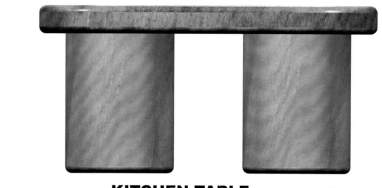

KITCHEN TABLE

STOVE

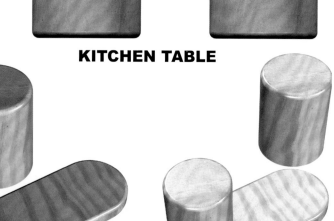

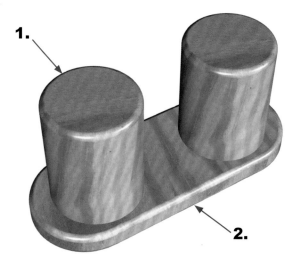

1. Glue table bases to table top. **2.** Let dry completely. Use actual size illustration below as guide for placement of table bases.

1.

2.

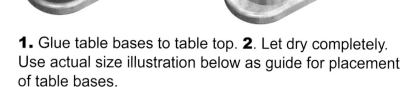

COPY THIS PATTERN FOR SAW GUIDE

1. TABLE BASE
(2) 1/2" dia. X 1-1/4"
DOWEL

2. TABLE TOP
(1) 1/4" X 1-1/4" X 3-1/8"
PINE

ACTUAL SIZE

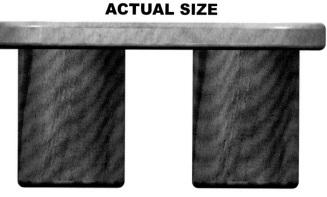

STOVE

Toddler's Toy Townhouse Kitchen Furnishings

FULL SIZE PATTERNS PAGES 23-25

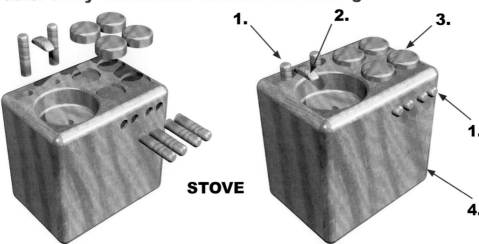

STOVE

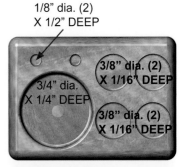

1/8" dia. (2)
X 1/2" DEEP

3/8" dia. (2)
X 1/16" DEEP

3/4" dia.
X 1/4" DEEP

3/8" dia. (2)
X 1/16" DEEP

COPY THIS
PATTERN FOR
SAW AND
DRILL GUIDE

1/8" dia. (4)
X 5/8" DEEP

1. Add a small spot of glue to each drilled hole in the stove base. Add a spot of glue to the bottom of the faucet.

2. Press faucet, handles and hot plates into place on the stove base. Let dry before handling the toy.

1. HANDLES (6)
1/8" diameter X 3/4"
DOWEL

2. FAUCET (1)
3/16" X 3/16" X 9/16"
PINE

3. HOT PLATES (4)
1/8" X 3/8" diameter
DOWEL

4. STOVE BASE (1)
1-1/2" X 1-3/4" X 1-3/4"
PINE

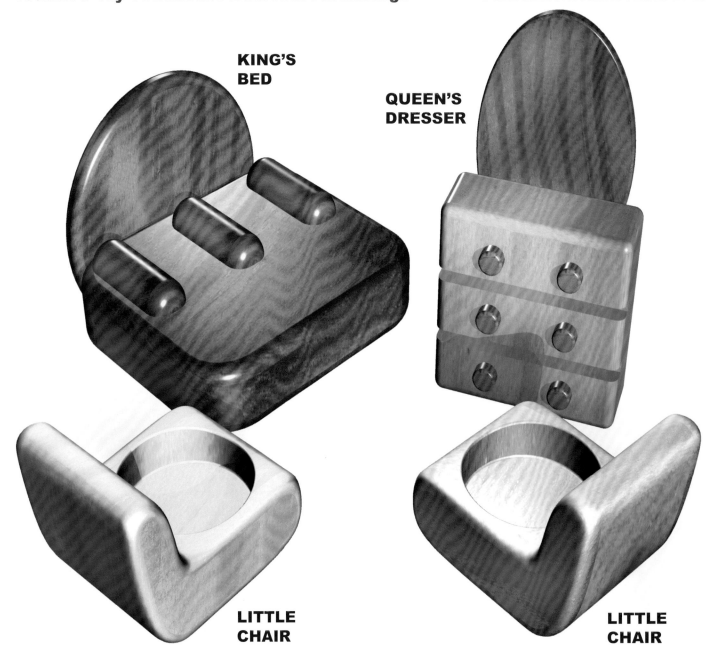

KING'S BED

QUEEN'S DRESSER

LITTLE CHAIR

LITTLE CHAIR

APPLYING FINISHING TOUCHES TO THE BEDROOM FURNISHINGS.

The Toddler's Toy Townhouse bedroom furnishings are designed to be finished in natural wood or in bright toddler's colors.

For a natural wood look apply clear, non-toxic polyurethane. Sand parts with a fine grit sandpaper. Lightly sand first coat then apply 2 coats sanding between each. Following the final coat rub lightly steel wool for a soft feel.

Bright colors can be applied using non-toxic acrylic paints as solid colors or thinned to apply as a wash or stain prior assembly.

Do not apply paint to gluing surfaces.

First sand all parts with a fine grit sandpaper. Apply first coat, let it dry thoroughly. Sand first coat then apply 2 coats sanding between each. Following assembly rub the each furnishing with steel wool for a soft to the surfaces.

HANDY TIP: For clean separation of stains when making a multi-colored wood toy use a wood burning stylus to mark the outline of the colors. This technique seal-burns the wood fibers and prevents paints and stains from bleeding into each other.

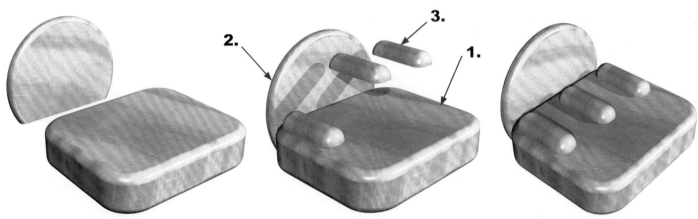

1. Add glue to the headboard and press tightly into place on mattress. Let assembly dry.

2. Add glue to each of 3 pillows and press each of the pillows into place as shown.

3. The bed looks great in plain wood or finished with stains or bright colors.

KING'S BED

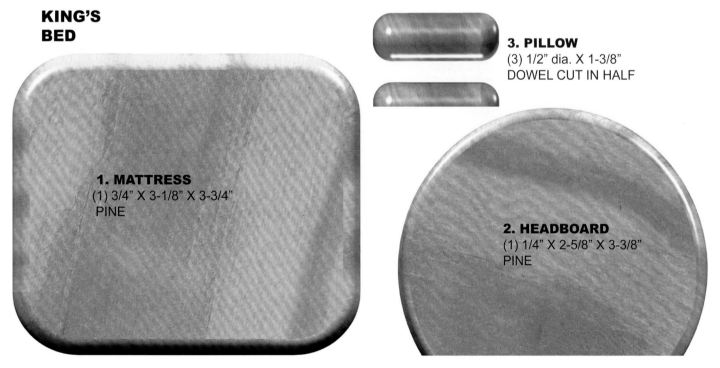

3. PILLOW
(3) 1/2" dia. X 1-3/8"
DOWEL CUT IN HALF

1. MATTRESS
(1) 3/4" X 3-1/8" X 3-3/4"
PINE

2. HEADBOARD
(1) 1/4" X 2-5/8" X 3-3/8"
PINE

QUEEN'S DRESSER

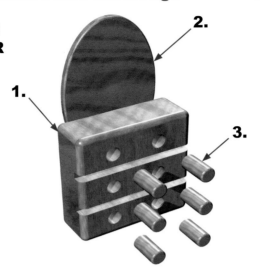

2.

1.

3.

1. Add glue to the mirror ellipse and press tightly into place on dresser. Let dry.

2. Add glue to each of 6 handle holes and press each of the handles tightly into place.

3. Dresser looks great in plain wood or finished.

It is fun to experiment with adding colors and textures to the townhouse furnishings. Solid colors, stains and texture paints add a dimension of fun, especially when the toddlers get to participate.

HANDLE HOLES
(6) 1/4" diameter
X 3/8" DEEP

DRAWER GROOVES
(2) 1/8" wide
X 1/8" DEEP SAW CUT

1. DRESSER
(1) 3/4" X 2" X 2"
PINE

2. MIRROR
(1) 1/4" X 1-3/4" X 2-3/4"
PINE

3. HANDLES
(6) 1/4" dia. X 1/2"
DOWEL

COPY PATTERNS FOR SAW AND DRILL GUIDE

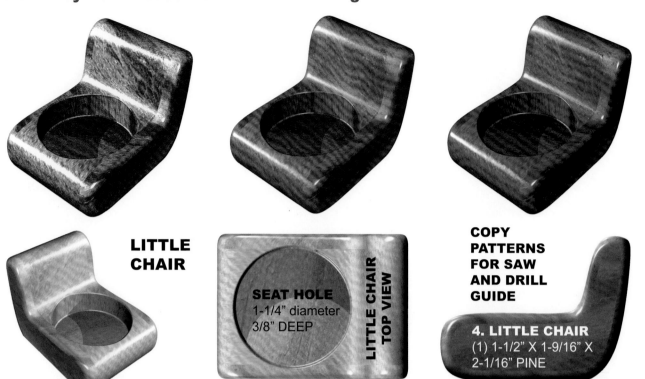

LITTLE CHAIR

SEAT HOLE
1-1/4" diameter
3/8" DEEP

LITTLE CHAIR TOP VIEW

COPY PATTERNS FOR SAW AND DRILL GUIDE

4. LITTLE CHAIR
(1) 1-1/2" X 1-9/16" X 2-1/16" PINE

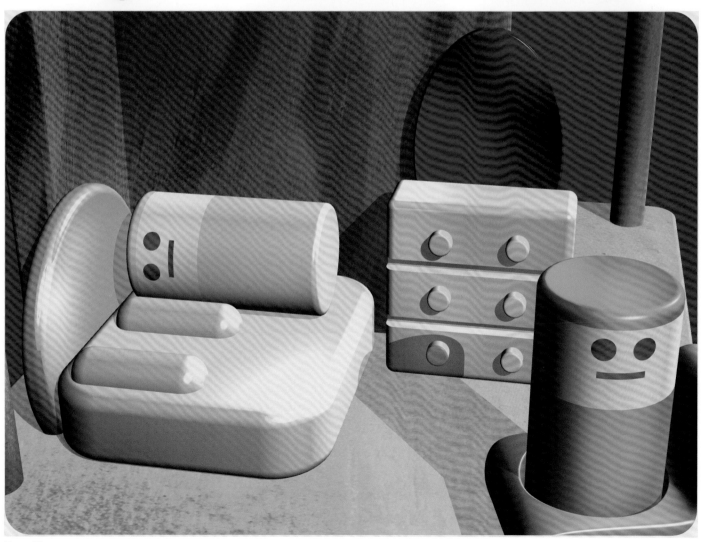

BATHROOM VIEW

VANITY

SHOWER

TOILET

APPLYING FINISHES TO THE BATHROOM FIXTURES AND FURNISHINGS.

The Toddler's Toy Townhouse bathroom fixtures and furnishings are designed to be finished in natural wood or in bright toddler's colors.

For a natural wood look apply clear, non-toxic polyurethane. Sand parts with a fine grit sandpaper. Lightly sand first coat then apply 2 coats sanding between each. Following the final coat rub lightly steel wool for a soft feel.

Bright colors can be applied using non-toxic acrylic paints as solid colors or thinned to apply as a wash or stain prior assembly.

Do not apply paint to gluing surfaces.

First sand all parts with a fine grit sandpaper. Apply first coat, let it dry thoroughly. Sand first coat then apply 2 coats sanding between each. Following assembly rub the bathroom furnishings with steel wool for a soft to the touch feel to the surfaces.

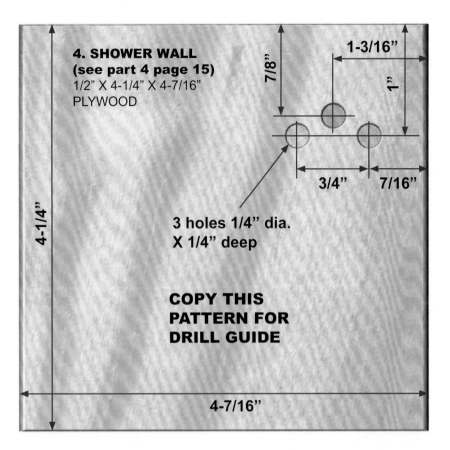

4. SHOWER WALL
(see part 4 page 15)
1/2" X 4-1/4" X 4-7/16"
PLYWOOD

7/8"

1-3/16"

1"

3/4"   7/16"

3 holes 1/4" dia.
X 1/4" deep

COPY THIS
PATTERN FOR
DRILL GUIDE

4-1/4"

4-7/16"

DRAIN HOLE
(1) 9/16" dia. X 3/16" DEEP

1. SHOWER BASE
(1) 1/2" X 2" X 2"
PINE

2. NOZZLE
(1) 1/4" dia. X 13/16"
DOWEL

3. HANDLE
(2) 1/4" dia. X 3/8"
DOWEL

SHOWER WALL DETAILS ARE ALSO SHOWN WITH PART 4 PAGE 15.

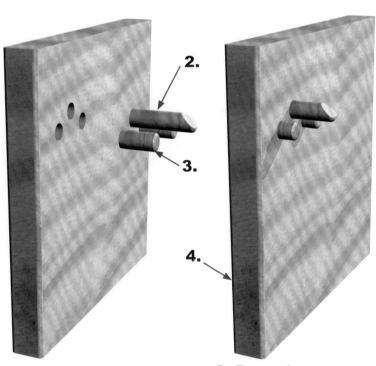

2.

3.

4.

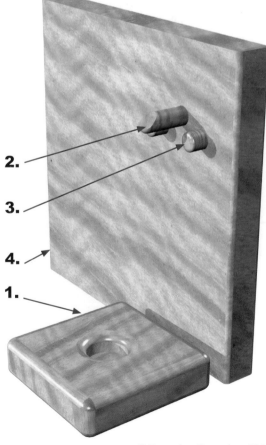

2.

3.

4.

1.

1. Add glue to the
handle holes in the
shower panel.

2. Press shower
handles into place
and let dry.

TOILET

1. Add glue to the toilet tank and press tightly into place on toilet bowl back. Let dry.

2. Add glue to the handle hole and press the handle tightly into place.

3. Assembled toilet is ideal for plain wood or decorative fun finishes.

TOILET BOWL
1-1/4" dia. X
1/2" DEEP

TOILET BOWL
(1) 3/4" X 1-1/2" X 1-5/8"
PINE

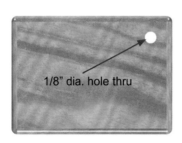

1/8" dia. hole thru

TOILET TANK
(1) 1/4" X 1-1/4" X 1-3/4"
PINE

TOILET HANDLE
(1) 1/8" dia. X 1/2"
DOWEL

COPY PATTERN FOR SAW AND DRILL GUIDE

VANITY

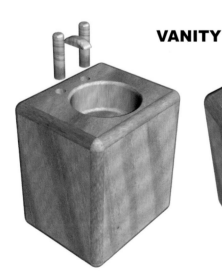 

VANITY
1-5/8" X 2" X 2-1/4"
PINE

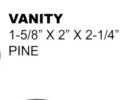

FAUCET (1)
3/16" X 3/16" X 9/16"
PINE

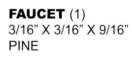

VANITY HANDLE
(2) 1/8" dia. X 3/4"
DOWEL

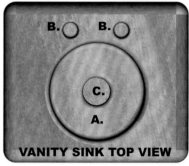

B. ○   B. ○

C.

A.

VANITY SINK TOP VIEW

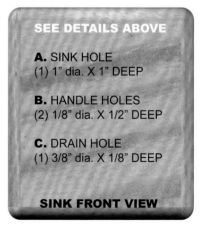

SEE DETAILS ABOVE

A. SINK HOLE
(1) 1" dia. X 1" DEEP

B. HANDLE HOLES
(2) 1/8" dia. X 1/2" DEEP

C. DRAIN HOLE
(1) 3/8" dia. X 1/8" DEEP

SINK FRONT VIEW

1. Add glue to the handles and faucet. Press tightly into place.

2. Assembled vanity is ideal for plain wood or decorative fun finishes.

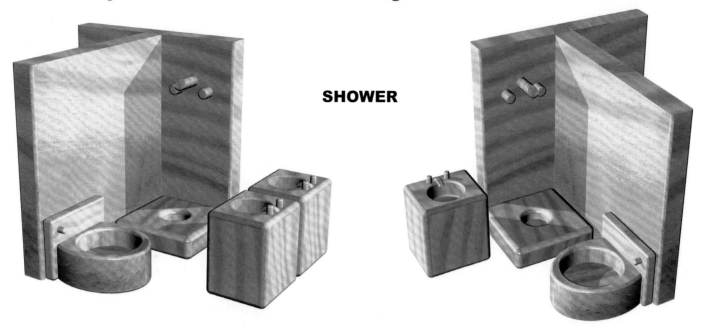

SHOWER

Make 2 or 3 of each of the townhouse furnishings. Toddlers love the chance to creatively decorate and arrange the toddler's townhouse to fit their imagination.

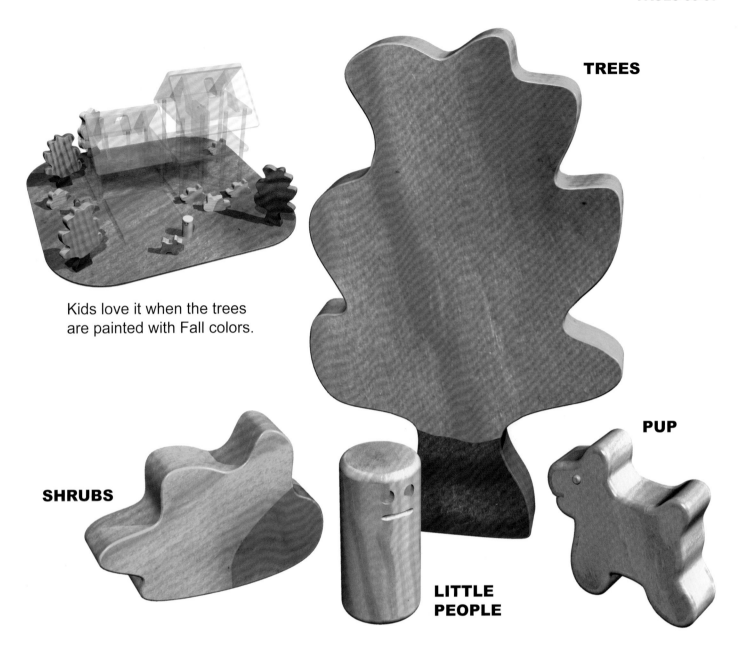

Kids love it when the trees are painted with Fall colors.

TREES

SHRUBS

PUP

LITTLE PEOPLE

APPLYING FINISHES TO THE TREES, SHRUBS, LITTLE PEOPLE AND PUP.

The Toddler's Toy Townhouse trees, shrubs, pup and little people are designed to be finished in natural wood or in bright toddler's colors. Trees also look great painted with bright Fall colors.

For a natural wood look apply clear, non-toxic polyurethane. Sand parts with a fine grit sandpaper. Lightly sand first coat then apply 2 coats sanding between each. Following the final coat rub lightly steel wool for a soft feel.

Bright colors can be applied using non-toxic acrylic paints as solid colors or thinned to apply as a wash or stain prior assembly.

Do not apply paint to gluing surfaces.

First sand all parts with a fine grit sandpaper. Apply first coat, let it dry thoroughly. Sand first coat then apply 2 coats sanding between each. Following assembly rub the finished toys with steel wool for a soft to the touch feel.

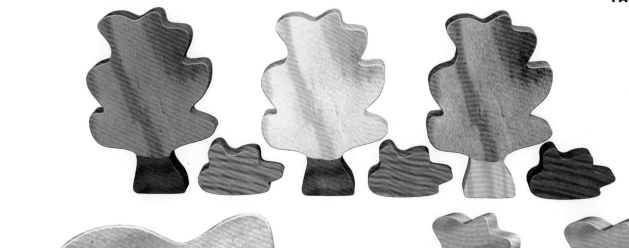

Glue base
to tree
for added
stability.

**FULL SIZE
TREE PATTERN**
3/4" X 4-3/4" X 7"
PINE

**FULL SIZE
TREE BASE
PATTERN**
1/4" X 2-1/2" X 2-1/2"
PINE

**FULL SIZE
SHRUB PATTERN**
3/4" X 2" X 3-1/4"
PINE

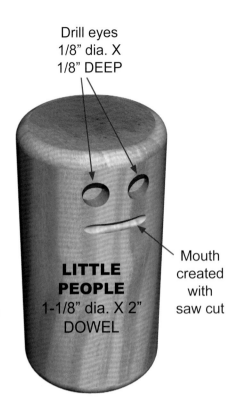

Drill eyes
1/8" dia. X
1/8" DEEP

**LITTLE
PEOPLE**
1-1/8" dia. X 2"
DOWEL

Mouth
created
with
saw cut

HANDY TIP: For clean separation of stains when making a hand painted multi-colored wood toy use a wood burning stylus to mark the outline of the colors. This technique seal-burns the wood fibers and prevents paints and stains from bleeding into each other.

PAINT DIPPING METHOD: A perfect finish can be created using solid color paints by carefully dipping the little people into a thinned solution of paint.

PAINT DIPPING STEPS:
1. Drive a finish nail into bottom of toy then bend the end into the shape of a hook with needle-nose pliers. Use the hook to dip the toy and for hang drying.
2. Dip one solid coat of the pants color on all of toy as a primer. Sand lightly.
3. Dip the toy into the face coat color to the required depth to create the face.
4. Dip the toy into the hat color to the required depth to create the hat.
5. Use a small brush to add the eyes and mouth.

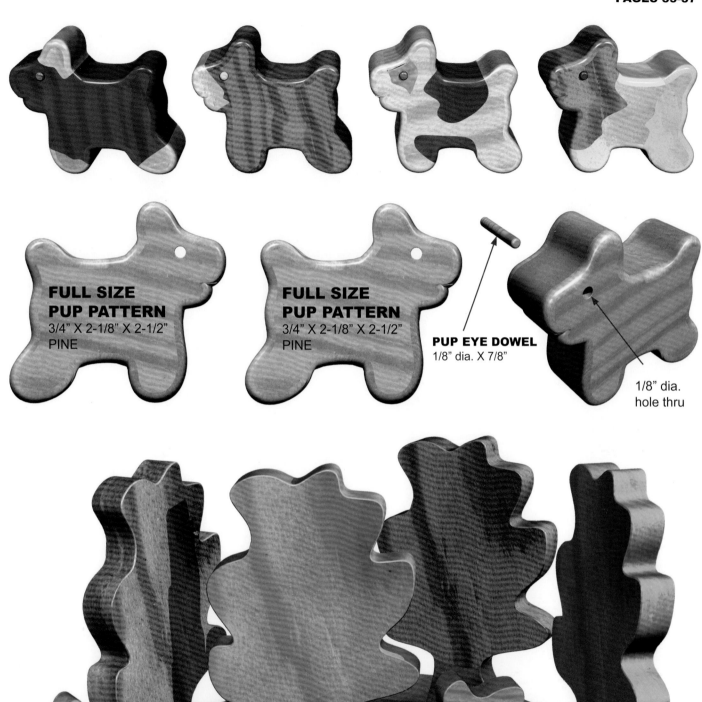

FULL SIZE PUP PATTERN
3/4" X 2-1/8" X 2-1/2"
PINE

FULL SIZE PUP PATTERN
3/4" X 2-1/8" X 2-1/2"
PINE

PUP EYE DOWEL
1/8" dia. X 7/8"

1/8" dia.
hole thru

Toddler's Toy Townhouse Sports Car and Little People

FULL SIZE PATTERNS PAGES 40-41

ACTUAL SIZE

Toddler's Toy Townhouse Sports Car

FULL SIZE PATTERNS PAGES 40-41

SPORTS CAR PARTS LIST

1. CAR CHASSIS	(1)	1-1/2" X 3-1/2" X 4-5/8"	PINE
2. WINDSHIELD	(1)	7/8" X 13/16" X 3-5/16"	PINE
3. HEAD/TAIL LIGHTS	(4)	1/8" X 3/8" X 3/4"	PINE
4. BUMPERS	(2)	1/4" X 5/8" X 3-5/16"	PINE
5. WHEELS	(4)	1-1/4" dia. X 3/4"	DOWEL
6. AXLE PEGS	(4)	Shaft 15/64" dia. for 1/4" hole X 1-3/8" long	PURCHASE

1. Glue front and rear lights and bumpers into position and let dry.

2. Glue the windshield into position and let dry before proceeding.

3. Slide axle pegs through wheels and glue axle pegs into chassis.

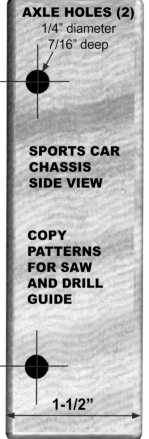

50 DEGREES

AXLE HOLES (2)
1/4" diameter
7/16" deep

SPORTS CAR CHASSIS SIDE VIEW

COPY PATTERNS FOR SAW AND DRILL GUIDE

1-1/2"

2. SPORTS CAR WINDSHIELD
(1) 7/8" X 13/16" X 3-5/16" PINE

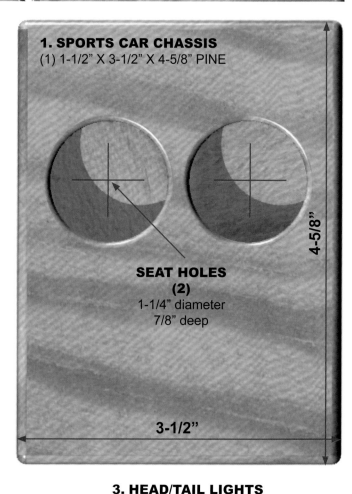

1. SPORTS CAR CHASSIS
(1) 1-1/2" X 3-1/2" X 4-5/8" PINE

SEAT HOLES (2)
1-1/4" diameter
7/8" deep

4-5/8"

3-1/2"

3. HEAD/TAIL LIGHTS
(4) 1/8" X 3/8" X 3/4" PINE

4. BUMPERS
(2) 1/4" X 5/8" X 3-5/16" PINE

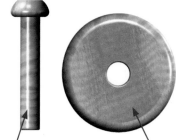

6. AXLE PEGS
(4) Shaft 15/64" dia. for 1/4" hole X 1-3/8" long PURCHASE

5. WHEELS
(4) 1-1/4" dia. X 3/4" DOWEL 9/32" dia. axle hole.

TOY AXLE PEGS CAN BE PURCHASED ONLINE FROM SEVERAL WEBSITES.

Toddler's Toy Townhouse Sports Car

FULL SIZE PATTERNS PAGES 40-41

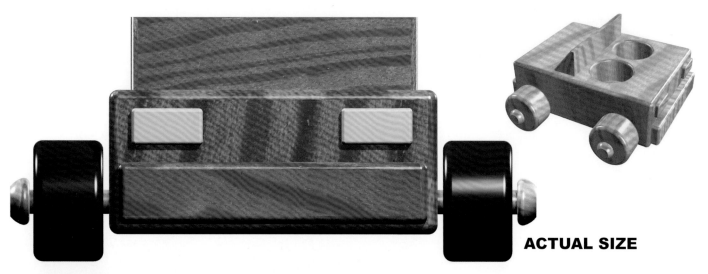

ACTUAL SIZE

Toddler's Toy Townhouse Detached Garage

1. Glue posts to floor.   2. Glue 2nd floor to posts.   3. Glue gables to floor.   4. Glue rear roof to gables.   5. Glue front roof to gables..   6. Completed.

DETACHED GARAGE PARTS LIST
1. POST (6) Same as part 6 page 15.
2. DRIVEWAY (1) Same as part 3 page 14.
3. 1ST, 2ND FLOOR (1 ea.) Same as part 2 page 13.
4. LANDSCAPE (1) Same as part 8 page 16.
5. GABLE (2) Same as part 7 page 17.
6. ROOFS (2) Same as parts 1 and 11 page 12.

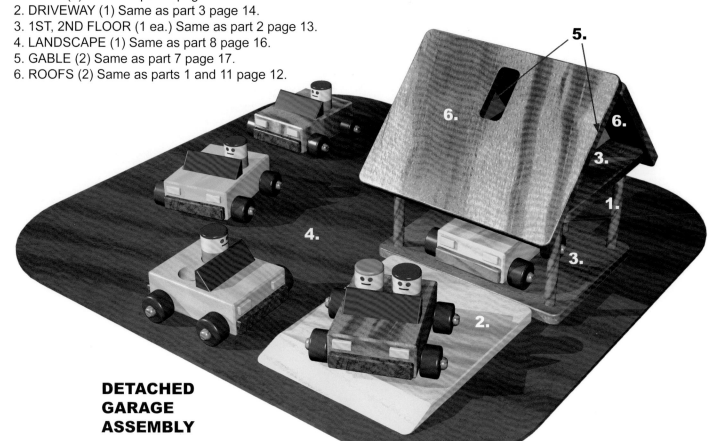

DETACHED GARAGE ASSEMBLY

ACTUAL SIZE

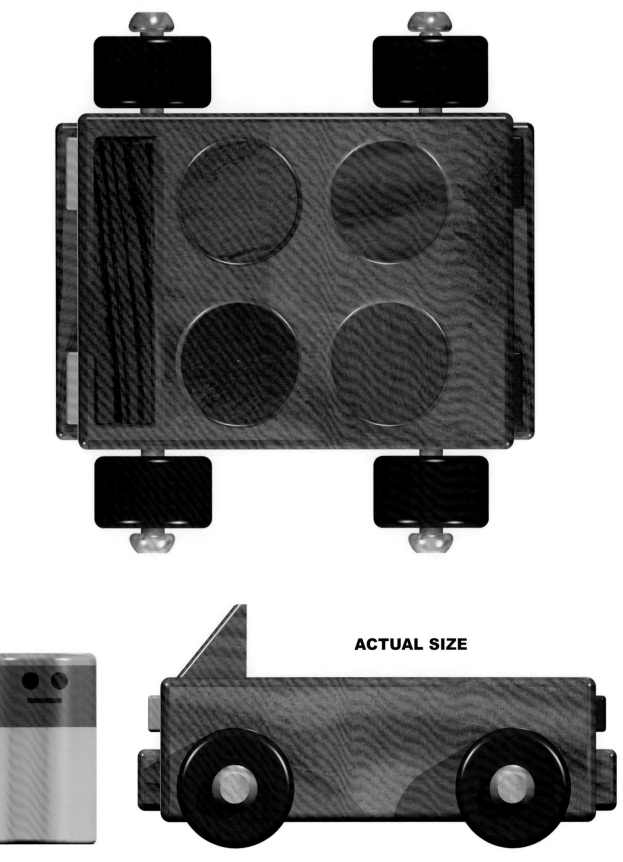

ACTUAL SIZE

Toddler's Toy Townhouse Mini Van and Little People

FULL SIZE PATTERNS PAGES 44-45

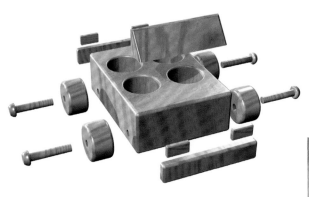

MINIVAN PARTS LIST

1. MINI VAN CHASSIS	(1)	1-1/2" X 3-1/2" X 4-5/8"	PINE
2. WINDSHIELD	(1)	7/8" X 13/16" X 3-5/16"	PINE
3. HEAD/TAIL LIGHTS	(4)	1/8" X 3/8" X 3/4"	PINE
4. BUMPERS	(2)	1/4" X 5/8" X 3-5/16"	PINE
5. WHEELS	(4)	1-1/4" diameter X 3/4"	DOWEL
6. AXLE PEGS	(4)	Shaft 15/64" dia. for 1/4" hole X 1-3/8" long	PURCHASE

50 DEGREES

2. MINI VAN WINDSHIELD
(1) 7/8" X 13/16" X 3-5/16" PINE

1. Glue front and rear lights and bumpers into position and let dry.

2. Glue the windshield into position and let dry before proceeding.

3. Slide axle pegs through wheels and glue axle pegs into chassis.

AXLE HOLES
(2) 1/4" dia. X 7/16" DEEP

MINIVAN CHASSIS SIDE VIEW

COPY PATTERNS FOR SAW AND DRILL GUIDE

1-1/2"

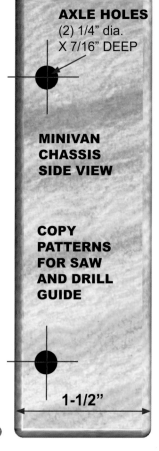

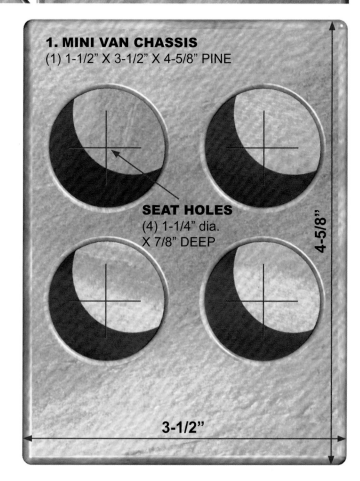

1. MINI VAN CHASSIS
(1) 1-1/2" X 3-1/2" X 4-5/8" PINE

SEAT HOLES
(4) 1-1/4" dia. X 7/8" DEEP

4-5/8"

3-1/2"

6. AXLE PEGS
(4) Shaft 15/64" dia. for 1/4" hole X 1-3/8" long PURCHASE

5. WHEELS
(4) 1-1/4" diameter X 3/4" DOWEL 9/32" dia. axle hole.

3. HEAD/TAIL LIGHTS
(4) 1/8" X 3/8" X 3/4" PINE

4. BUMPERS
(2) 1/4" X 5/8" X 3-5/16" PINE

TOY AXLE PEGS CAN BE PURCHASED ONLINE FROM SEVERAL WEBSITES.

Toddler's Toy Townhouse Mini Van and Little People

FULL SIZE PATTERNS
PAGES 44-45

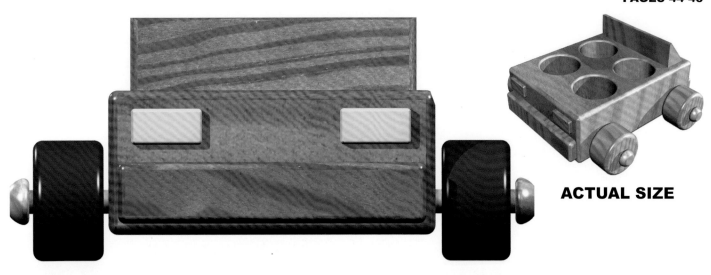

ACTUAL SIZE

Toddler's Toy Townhouse Carport

1. Glue posts to floor.

2. Glue walls to floor.

3. Glue roof to posts and wall.

4. Completed carport.

CARPORT PARTS LIST
1. DRIVEWAY (1): Same as part 3 page 14.
2. ROOF, FLOOR (1 ea.): Same as part 2 page 13.
3. WALL (2): Same as part 4 page 15.
4. POST (6): Same as part 6 page 15.

CARPORT ASSEMBLY

Toddler's Toy Townhouse Gas Station Assembly

FULL SIZE PATTERNS PAGES 46-47

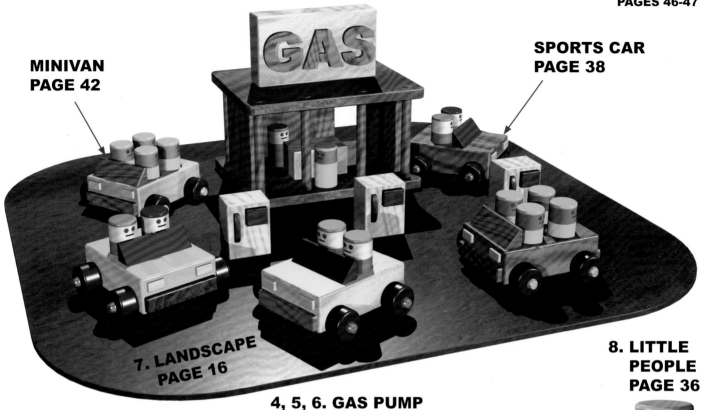

MINIVAN PAGE 42

SPORTS CAR PAGE 38

7. LANDSCAPE PAGE 16

8. LITTLE PEOPLE PAGE 36

4, 5, 6. GAS PUMP

2. CASH COUNTER

1,3. STATION SIGN

GAS STATION PARTS LIST

1. SIGNBOARD	(1) 1-1/2" X 3-1/2" X 6-1/2"	PINE
2. CASH COUNTER	(1) 1-1/2" X 2" X 3"	PINE
3. GAS SIGN: Scroll saw from 1/8" X 2" X 6" material.		
4. GAS PUMP	(1) 1-1/2" X 2-3/8" X 3"	PINE
5. GAS HOSE	(1) 1" X 1-1/4" X 1/4"	PINE
6. PUMP READOUT	(1) 1" X 1-1/4" X 1/4"	PINE
7. LANDSCAPE (1): Same as part 8 page 16.		
8. LITTLE PEOPLE: Same as little people, page 36.		
9. ROOF, FLOOR (1 ea.): Same as part 2 page 13.		
10. WALL (2): Same as part 4 page 15.		
11. POST (6): Same as part 6 page 15.		

GAS STATION

1. Glue posts to floor.   2. Glue walls to floor.   3. Glue roof to posts, wall.   4. Glue sign in place.

3. GAS SIGN: Scroll saw from 1/8" X 2" X 6" material.

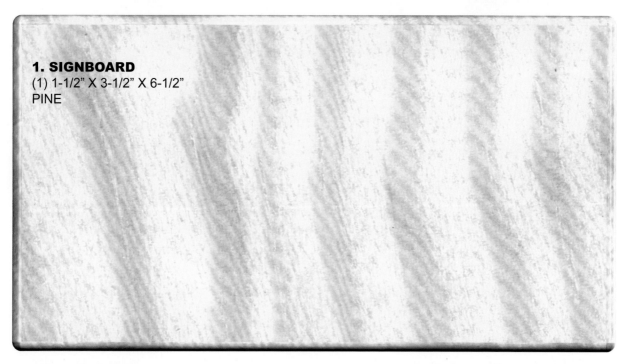

1. SIGNBOARD
(1) 1-1/2" X 3-1/2" X 6-1/2"
PINE

2. CASH COUNTER
(1) 1-1/2" X 2" X 3"
PINE

6. PUMP READOUT
(1) 1" X 1-1/4" X 1/4"
PINE

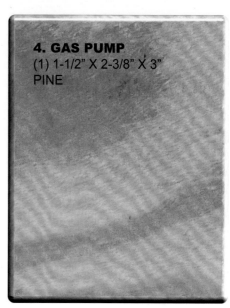

4. GAS PUMP
(1) 1-1/2" X 2-3/8" X 3"
PINE

5. GAS HOSE
(1) 1" X 1-1/4" X 1/4"
PINE

DETACHED GARAGE PLAY SET PAGE 41

TODDLER'S TOWNHOUSE PLAY SET PAGE 4

CARPORT PLAY SET PAGE 45

GAS STATION PLAY SET PAGE 46

GAS